SMALL-GAME HUNTING

by Tom Carpenter

Content Consultant
Bill Sherck
Outdoor Television Show Host

SportsZone

An Imprint of Abdo Publishing
abdopublishing.com

abdopublishing.com

Published by Abdo Publishing, a division of ABDO, PO Box 398166, Minneapolis, Minnesota 55439. Copyright © 2016 by Abdo Consulting Group, Inc. International copyrights reserved in all countries. No part of this book may be reproduced in any form without written permission from the publisher. SportsZone™ is a trademark and logo of Abdo Publishing.

Printed in the United States of America, North Mankato, Minnesota
052015
092015

Cover Photos: Andreas Zerndl/Shutterstock Images (background); Herbert Kratky/Shutterstock Images (foreground)
Interior Photos: Andreas Zerndl/Shutterstock Images, 1 (background); Herbert Kratky/Shutterstock Images, 1 (foreground); Shutterstock Images, 4–5, 6; Kirn Vintage Stock/Corbis, 8; iStockphoto, 10–11, 14, 20, 32 (top); Lynn Bystrom/ Stockphoto, 17; Carolyn Kaster/AP Images, 18–19; Douglas Graham/WLP Inc./Newscom, 23; Tyler Olson/Shutterstock Images, 24; Michael Pearce/ TNS/Newscom, 26; Stockbyte/Thinkstock, 28–29, 43; Jesse A. Wanskasmith/ Newscom, 30; Petr Malyshev/iStockphoto, 32 (bottom); Dale Spartas/Corbis, 34–35; Sascha Burkard/Shutterstock Images, 36; Arina P. Habich/Shutterstock Images, 38; Glow Images, 40–41; Kevin Horan/Corbis, 44

Editor: Jon Westmark
Series Designer: Jake Nordby

Library of Congress Control Number: 2015931753

Cataloging-in-Publication Data
Carpenter, Tom.
Small-game hunting / Tom Carpenter.
  p. cm. -- (Hunting)
Includes bibliographical references and index.
ISBN 978-1-62403-836-5
1. Small game hunting--Juvenile literature. 2. Fowling--Juvenile literature.
I. Title.
799.2/5--dc23

                                                        2015931753

CONTENTS

Chapter 1

WELCOME TO SMALL-GAME HUNTING   4

Chapter 2

BIOLOGY AND HABITAT   10

Chapter 3

TECHNIQUES   18

Chapter 4

EQUIPMENT AND SKILLS   28

Chapter 5

SAFETY AND CONSERVATION   40

Glossary...46
For More Information...47
Index...48
About the Author...48

WELCOME TO SMALL-GAME HUNTING

A boy and his sister enter a forest near their home. The October sun is warm. The sky is blue. The trees are covered in yellow, orange, and red leaves. The young hunters sneak to a

In many states, small-game hunting opens in early fall and lasts into winter.

wide oak tree. They load their .22 caliber rifles. Then the siblings sit down on opposite sides of the tree and quietly watch their surroundings.

After a long wait, the boy sees movement in the tree limbs. A big, speckled gray squirrel sits

Squirrels can be found in the woods at any time of day. But they are most active in the morning.

on a tree limb only 20 yards (18 m) away. The boy takes careful aim. *Crack!* At the sound of the shot, the squirrel falls to the ground. The hunters get up to claim their trophy.

A month later, a light dusting of snow covers the area around the siblings' home. This time the young hunters are in an area of thickets filled with brush, grass, weeds, and thorny raspberry branches. They are looking for cottontail rabbits.

Suddenly a rabbit runs out of a brushy tangle. It looks like a streak of gray. But the white snow helps the girl see the animal. She swings her shotgun, makes sure the shot is safe, and pulls the trigger.

Boom! The rabbit skids to a stop in the snow. The young hunter walks over and picks up the animal. She admires it for a moment before putting it in the game bag of her hunting vest. The hunters continue walking in search of more cottontails.

Small Game through History

Small-game hunting has a long history in North America. Native Americans hunted small game using bows and arrows, traps, and snares.

Rabbits and other small game provide lean meat for hunters and their families.

The earliest settlers from Europe hunted small game to feed their families. Squirrels were a favorite target. Forests covered much of North America in the 1600s. It was thought that a squirrel could travel from the Atlantic Ocean to the Mississippi River without coming down from trees. Squirrels were plentiful in the massive habitat.

Settlers began logging forests and creating farms. This produced areas of young brush, which rabbits inhabit. Rabbit populations increased.

Raccoons thrived in the changing environment too. Farm fields offered new sources of food for raccoons, and plenty of woods remained for the raccoons to hide in during the day.

Through the late 1800s and into the early 1900s, small-game hunting was a tradition for many families. It was an important way to put meat on the table.

Today most people do not depend on the game they hunt. But small-game hunting is still a great way for young hunters to learn important hunting skills, to have fun, and to provide meals for their families.

Chapter 2

BIOLOGY AND HABITAT

In order to be a successful small-game hunter, it is important to understand the game's habitat and behavior. This knowledge helps the hunter be in the right place at the right time to

Small-game animals may be common, but they can be difficult to hunt.

shoot small game. Some people hunt coyotes, bobcats, and foxes in North America. But the most popular small-game targets are squirrels, rabbits, and raccoons. These animals have healthy populations across the continent.

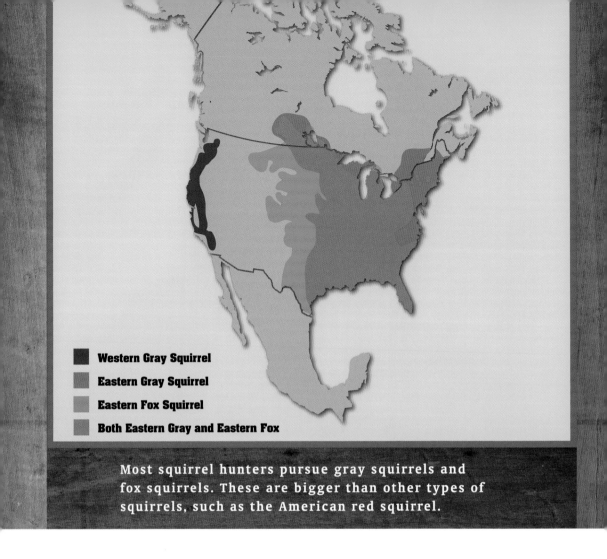

Western Gray Squirrel
Eastern Gray Squirrel
Eastern Fox Squirrel
Both Eastern Gray and Eastern Fox

Most squirrel hunters pursue gray squirrels and fox squirrels. These are bigger than other types of squirrels, such as the American red squirrel.

Squirrels

Gray squirrels are the most common and widespread type of squirrel in North America. Hunters may find gray squirrels in small patches of woods or large forests. Gray squirrels prefer woodlands with nut trees such as oak, hickory, and walnut.

Gray squirrels measure 14 to 21 inches (36–53 cm) in length. They weigh up to 1 1/2 pounds (0.7 kg). As their name describes, most of their fur is gray. But they have white bellies. Some gray squirrels also have rust-colored fur fringes around their stomachs and on their ears. Gray squirrels eat nuts, berries, mushrooms, and crops such as corn.

Many areas in North America also have fox squirrels. Fox squirrels live in forests too. But fox squirrels are not as common in deep or thick woods. Fox squirrels often live in wooded pastures, small groves of trees, and other areas with few trees.

Fox squirrels are named for their rust-orange fur. Their undersides are creamy orange or yellow. Their backs and sides are a salt-and-pepper color with a red or orange tinge. Their tails are orange-gray. Fox squirrels are big. They measure 19 to 30 inches (48–76 cm) from nose to

Snowshoe hares' huge feet help them run across snow without sinking in.

tail and weigh up to 2 3/4 pounds (1.2 kg). Fox squirrels eat nuts, berries, and crops.

Both gray squirrels and fox squirrels have excellent eyes and ears. When they see or hear danger coming, they run to their hole or nest, or they stay motionless on a limb to let danger pass.

Cottontail Rabbits

Various types of cottontail rabbits live across North America. Cottontails live in places where there is a lot of cover low to the ground. Tall grasses and weeds, thick forest edges, hedgerows, and thickets may all hold cottontails.

Cottontails measure 14 to 19 inches (36–48 cm) in length. They weigh from 2 to 3 1/2 pounds (0.9–1.6 kg). Their fur ranges from gray to rusty brown. Their undersides are creamy white. The underside of their tails is bright white, making the tail look like a ball of cotton and giving the cottontail its name.

Cottontails feed mostly at night. They hide during the day, tucked into thick cover. Cottontails eat grasses, greens from young plants, fruits, berries, and

Snowshoe Hares

In far northern areas of the United States and into Canada and Alaska, hunters pursue snowshoe hares. Snowshoe hares are bigger than other rabbits. They measure between 16 and 20 inches (41–51 cm) and weigh up to 4 pounds (1.8 kg). Snowshoes have brown-gray fur much of the year. In the fall, their fur turns patchy brown-white, and then it turns all white for winter.

grains such as corn and soybeans. In winter they gnaw on the nutritious bark of young bushes.

Cottontails have excellent hearing and sight. When the rabbits sense danger approaching, they often freeze in place until it passes. But cottontails will run off quickly if danger gets too close.

Raccoons

Raccoons are very adaptable. They live in many kinds of habitat. Large forests, farm areas, mountains, foothills, and prairies all hold raccoons. Raccoons like to be near creeks, ponds, and other waterways.

Raccoons have gray-brown fur, black markings that look like a mask across their faces, and ringed tails. A full-grown male, or boar, may measure up to 40 inches (102 cm) and weigh 30 pounds (13.6 kg). Average boars are approximately 30 inches (76 cm) long and weigh up to 15 pounds (6.8 kg). Average females weigh from 10 to 12 pounds (4.5–5.4 kg).

Raccoons like to hunt for crayfish, frogs, and fish by waiting near the water's edge.

Raccoons feed at night. They are omnivores, which means they eat both plant and animal matter. Raccoons eat fruits, seeds, nuts, tender shoots and leaves, berries, and crops such as corn. They also eat fish, frogs, crayfish, insects, clams, grubs, and worms. Raccoons gain a lot of weight in the fall to prepare for a winter of inactivity.

Raccoons have excellent hearing and sight. They will run up a tree or swim down a creek to escape danger.

Chapter 3

TECHNIQUES

Small-game hunting is challenging. Successful hunters do not simply walk through the woods hoping to shoot game. They plan carefully and

Making a plan can help a group of hunters hunt more effectively and safely.

put specific hunting strategies and techniques to work.

Squirrel Hunting

Many people are familiar with squirrels in parks or residential areas. But squirrels living in wild

Some squirrel hunters walk slowly through the forest and look for squirrels to sneak up on.

areas are more careful and evasive than town squirrels. Wild squirrels can be challenging to hunt.

One hunting strategy is to find a place with a lot of squirrels, sneak into the area, and sit and wait. This way, when a squirrel appears, the hunter is ready to take a shot.

A good place to wait for squirrels is a wooded area with nut trees. Hunters sit down with their backs against trees. This breaks up their outlines, making them harder to see. They also wear camouflage to help them stay hidden. It is important to be still and quiet. Many squirrel hunters stay put for a while after shooting a squirrel because more squirrels may appear.

Another good way to hunt squirrels is by walking and stalking. In this type of hunt, hunters move slowly along through the woods. They stop often, sometimes at every tree. They lean against the tree to hide. After a few minutes, they move on to the next tree.

If the hunters spot a squirrel, they can follow it. It is a good idea to stay

Hunting with Squirrel Dogs

Some hunters use dogs to hunt squirrels. The hunter and dog walk through the forest. When the dog sees or smells a squirrel, it chases the squirrel up a tree. The dog stands there and barks until the hunter walks up to spot and shoot the squirrel. Many dog breeds can be trained to squirrel hunt.

behind trees while stalking. Hunters can also wait for squirrels to move toward them.

Squirrel hunters can be successful at any time of day. But for gray squirrels, the hours at dawn and evening are best. Grays are more active during these times. Fox squirrels become active at midmorning and continue moving around through late afternoon.

Hunting Rabbits with Hound Dogs

Many rabbit hunters keep one or more hound dogs for rabbit hunting. Beagles and basset hounds are great breeds for rabbit hunting. When a rabbit runs off, the hounds take chase. They howl and bawl as they track. Rabbits often run in a big circle and come back to the place they were flushed. The hunter waits there and shoots the rabbit when it comes back ahead of the dogs.

Rabbit Hunting

Cottontail rabbit hunters stay on the move. They might try to scare a rabbit and get it to run so they can shoot it. Or they might try to spot a cottontail while it is sitting still and shoot it before it runs.

Trying to flush rabbits to shoot them can take a lot of

A hunter and his beagles set out on a rabbit hunt. Beagles are great dogs for finding and chasing rabbits.

work. Hunters walk through thick, brushy habitats. They kick brush piles, shake downed trees, and generally try to get rabbits to run from their hiding places. These hunters carry shotguns. They must be ready to shoot any running rabbits.

Rabbit tracks are easy to spot in the snow. Rabbits' big hind legs make the front tracks, and their front paws make the rear tracks.

Some hunters stalk rabbits. Instead of trying to flush cottontails, hunters sneak through the habitat. They pause often, stopping to study the landscape closely and to look for rabbits. Cottontails have big black eyes that stand out. Their ears are also big and noticeable. Stalking is best when there is snow on the ground, because the rabbits are easier to spot. Most stalking hunters use rifles. They try to shoot stationary rabbits in the head. If a rabbit runs before the hunter has a shot, rifle hunters do not shoot. They wait for the rabbit to pause.

Raccoon Hunting

Raccoon hunting happens at night. That is when raccoons are most active.

Hunting Snowshoe Hares

Snowshoe hares tend to live in areas that get a lot of snow in the winter. Hunters put on skis or snowshoes and dress in white camouflage. They stalk along and look for movement. It can be difficult to see a white snowshoe hare in the snow. Hunters look for a hare's big black eyes or black ear tips.

A redbone coonhound leads its handler through the dark to a raccoon up a tree.

Hunters strap on headlamps and take their dogs out to woods and fields. When the dogs pick up the scent of a raccoon, they howl and chase the animal.

When the dogs start catching up with the raccoon, it will climb a tree. The hounds yip and yowl, guiding the hunters to the tree. One hunter uses a spotlight to locate the raccoon. This person shines the light down the barrel of a gun so a hunting partner can aim at and shoot the raccoon.

Good dogs for raccoon hunting include coonhounds, such as black-and-tans, blueticks, redbones, treeing walkers, and Plotts.

Hunters can pursue raccoons without dogs too. These hunters go out with spotlights along the edges of fields and woods. If a raccoon runs up a tree, the hunters shine their lights on it and shoot it.

Chapter 4

EQUIPMENT AND SKILLS

Small-game hunters must have the necessary equipment. Small-game gear is relatively simple and inexpensive. But hunters must know how to use their gear and use effective hunting

Many small-game firearms are good for beginner hunters to learn with.

techniques. These things can help hunters find success in the field.

Small-Game Equipment

A small-game hunter needs the right firearm. A .22-caliber rimfire rifle is ideal for small-game

A bolt-action rifle with a scope can help hunters hit their targets with better precision.

hunting. A .22 is a small rifle that shoots a small cartridge. It makes a soft crack when fired.

Bolt-action rifles are most accurate. Many small-game hunters put scopes on their rifles to make them even more accurate. Most hunters using .22s try to shoot their target in the head. A shot here kills the game instantly.

A squirrel head is not very big. And a rabbit or raccoon head is also hard to hit. Most successful small-game hunters practice a lot with their .22 rifles to become accurate shooters. When hunting, they find trees, rocks, or fence posts to lean against and steady their shots.

Squirrel hunters occasionally use shotguns. Rabbit hunters are more likely to use shotguns. Shotguns shoot many small pellets, or BBs, instead of a single bullet. A 20-gauge shotgun is the ideal size for small-game hunting. Larger 16- or 12-gauges also work.

Squirrel hunters prefer a full choke on the shotgun barrel. A choke controls how much the pellets spread out. A full choke concentrates the pellets in a tight pattern. Squirrels are tough to bring down, and it takes multiple pellets to do it.

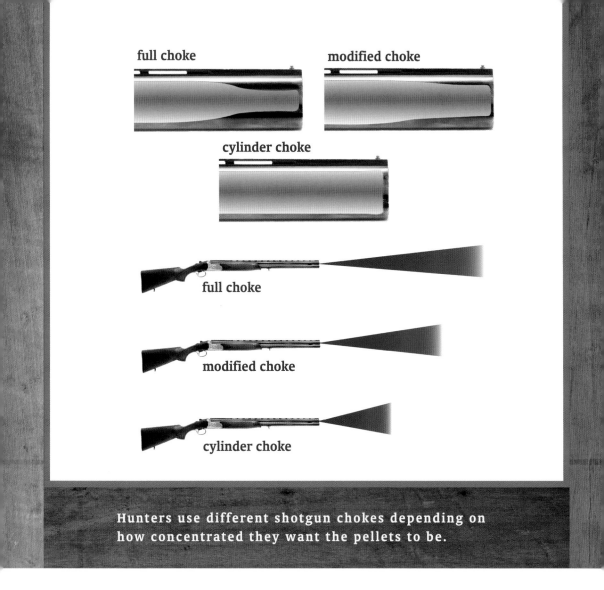

full choke

modified choke

cylinder choke

full choke

modified choke

cylinder choke

Hunters use different shotgun chokes depending on
how concentrated they want the pellets to be.

Rabbit hunters go with a more open shotgun choke to
get a wider pattern. This helps them hit running animals
with a pellet or two. Rabbits are easier to bring down than
squirrels. It only takes a couple of pellets to do it.

Small-game hunters dress simply. On warm days, regular clothes will do. Some hunters wear camouflage. Many wear an orange hat so that other hunters can see them. When it is cold, it is important to dress in layers that can be taken off as the day warms up. Good boots are important to keep feet warm and comfortable.

Squirrel hunters sometimes carry a squirrel call. When nothing is happening in the woods, they make a few squirrel sounds called cackles or chatters. This can get a real squirrel to call back and reveal its location. Many small-game hunters also carry a water bottle, snacks to keep them energized, and a hunting knife for field dressing game.

Small-Game Skills

Small-game hunting can be simple and fun. But most successful hunters put time into finding available places to hunt and scouting to see if there is game in the area.

SMALL-GAME EQUIPMENT

Shotgun: Shotguns allow hunters to cover larger areas with their shots.

Beagle: Beagles are energetic, determined dogs that help flush out small game for hunters to shoot.

Blaze Orange: Blaze orange helps hunters see one another.

Rifle: Rifles allow hunters to shoot at targets from farther away.

35

Many great hunting areas are on private land. It is important to gain permission before hunting on private land.

There are public lands where people can hunt small game. Some state game agencies lease private land for public hunting. State game department websites identify these lands and help hunters find them.

There is often great small-game hunting on private land too. Hunters need to get permission from the landowner to hunt in these areas. The best approach is to meet with the owner before hunting season starts and ask politely to use the land. Many landowners appreciate this approach and give permission to hunt.

After hunters find land to hunt on, they must scout to find where the game may be. Squirrel hunters look for woods with nut trees, especially oaks, hickories, and walnut trees. Hunters can listen for squirrels cackling and look for nutshells below a branch where a squirrel has eaten. Rabbit hunters look for thick, brushy areas where there are rabbit droppings on the ground.

Many small-game hunters practice shooting at small targets to become more steady and accurate.

Many small-game hunters practice during the summer with their rifles or shotguns. Rifle hunters use tiny targets to help them become more accurate. Shotgun hunters go trap shooting to practice shooting moving targets.

Many people enjoy the taste of squirrels, rabbits, hares, and raccoons. But first the hunter must field dress the game. It is important that hunters do this shortly after bagging their game to cool the meat and keep it from going bad. It is against the law to waste animal meat.

Squirrels are hardest to skin. Young hunters can get an adult to help them learn how. Rabbits are a bit easier. Their skin pulls off easily. Then the animal's organs are removed, and it is cut up into pieces to be cooked.

There are many great ways to cook small game. Squirrel is good roasted for a few hours on low heat. Rabbit is often fried like chicken. Another great way to prepare small game is to cook the meat in broth, remove the bones, and serve with barbecue sauce.

Chapter 5

SAFETY AND CONSERVATION

Small-game firearms are not usually as powerful as firearms used for larger game. But small-game rifles and shotguns can seriously injure people and property if used incorrectly.

Hunters in groups need to be especially careful when handling their firearms.

All hunters should take a firearms safety course to learn how to handle their guns safely and effectively. Most states require it.

It can be hard to remember safety rules when a rabbit or squirrel is darting away. But it is

TAB-K Formula

One good way to remember how to be safe with a firearm is by following the TAB-K formula:

T— Treat every firearm as if it were loaded at all times.

A— Always point the barrel of the gun in a safe direction.

B— Be certain of your target and what's beyond it.

K— Keep your finger outside of the trigger guard until you are ready to shoot.

especially important at these times for hunters to make sure they are being safe with their firearms.

Many small-game hunters wear blaze orange clothing on their upper bodies. This helps other hunters see them in the woods or brush. When hunting in a group, it is also a good idea to make and follow a plan to keep track of one another during the hunt. This helps hunters avoid shooting in one another's direction.

Licensing and Conservation

Hunters must have the proper small-game hunting licenses for their states. Many states offer free or low-cost

Hunting in pairs can be easy to coordinate and can increase the likelihood of bagging small game.

hunting licenses to young hunters. This encourages these hunters to get into the woods and enjoy small-game hunting.

Small-game hunters must also follow all rules related to open hunting seasons. Each state's hunting regulations

Small-game hunting is a great way to experience fall weather with friends and family.

booklet or website lists open season dates for squirrels, rabbits, and other small game.

Hunting seasons are an important conservation tool. Conservation is the wise use of natural resources. Small-game hunting seasons are held in fall and winter. These are times when squirrels, rabbits, and other small game are done raising their young for the year. Game populations would suffer if females with young were shot in spring and summer.

States also set bag limits that are different for each species of small game. This helps ensure that no one shoots too many animals in a day. A person can shoot different species of small game in the same day but only a certain number of each type of game.

For many hunters, small-game hunting is about more than shooting their limit. It is about time spent in nature, the thrill of the hunt, and the satisfaction of bringing home a meal to eat.

GLOSSARY

bolt-action rifle

A firearm with a hand-operated action that is pulled up and back to eject a cartridge and then pushed forward and down to load a new one.

caliber

The side-to-side measurement of the cartridge.

cartridge

A combination of primer, brass casing, powder, and bullet that is loaded into a rifle and fired.

flush

When an animal jumps from its hiding spot and runs off.

lease

An agreement between a game department and a landowner to allow public hunting on the landowner's land.

rifle

A firearm that shoots a cartridge. A cartridge has only one bullet that comes out of the end of the barrel.

rimfire

A cartridge that is fired by being struck on its edge instead of its center. Rimfire cartridges are simpler and tend to be less expensive than other cartridges.

shotgun

A type of firearm loaded with a shotgun shell consisting of primer, plastic casing, and a wad holding small metal balls called pellets.

trap shooting

A type of shotgun practice shooting in which clay targets are launched through the air.

FOR MORE INFORMATION

Further Reading

Crosby, Jeff, Shelley Ann Jackson. *Little Lions, Bull Baiters & Hunting Hounds: A History of Dog Breeds*. New York: Tundra Books, 2008.

Finne, Stephanie. *Beagles*. Minneapolis: Abdo Publishing, 2015.

Gurtler, Janet. *Small Game*. New York: AV2 by Weigl, 2013.

Websites

To learn more about Hunting, visit **booklinks.abdopublishing.com**. These links are routinely monitored and updated to provide the most current information available.

INDEX

blaze orange, 33, 35, 42

camouflage, 21, 25, 32

cartridge, 30

choke, 31–32

clothing, 32–33, 42

conservation, 44–45

cooking small game, 39

cottontail rabbit, 7, 14–16, 22–23, 25

dogs, 21, 22, 27, 34

field dress, 33, 39

fox squirrel, 12, 13–14, 22

gray squirrel, 5–6, 12–14, 22

hunting license, 42–43

hunting safety, 7, 40–42

hunting season, 37, 43–44

pellets, 31, 32

practice, 31, 39

private land, 37

raccoon, 9, 11, 16–17, 25, 27, 31, 39

rimfire rifle, 29

scope, 30–31

scout, 33, 37

shotgun, 7, 23, 31, 32, 34, 37, 39, 40

small-game habitat, 9, 10, 12, 13, 14–15, 16, 23, 25

small-game senses, 14, 16, 17

snowshoe hare, 15, 25

spotlight, 27

squirrel call, 33

stalking, 21–22, 25

TAB-K, 42

.22 caliber rifle, 5, 29–31

ABOUT THE AUTHOR

Tom Carpenter is a father, a sportsman, and an outdoor writer. He has introduced many children, including his three sons, to the thrills and rewards of hunting. A native son of Wisconsin who always has part of his heart in South Dakota, he planted roots in the middle. He lives with his family near the shores of Bass Lake, Minnesota.